I0152710

God Speaks, Daily

Big Things Happen With the God Who Speaks - Life-Changing Stories

Marvine J. Davis

Published by:

ISBN: 978-1-958404-57-7 (paperback)

Acknowledgment

In loving memory of my mother, Evadne Ruddock, who taught me how to hear and identify the voice of God.

With all my love.

Table of Contents

Introduction

"His Word is not a chore. Not a nag. It's life. It's love. It's living truth, solid as granite yet soft as a baby's skin. And it's not just to read. It's to absorb. To bathe in. To live by. To inspire us, reshape us, and define us." —Priscilla Shirer

*I*t has always been a thought that has stuck with me over the years, that when I leave this life, I must leave empty. I would have done all that God have purposed for me to do.

It is for that reason I acknowledge that as I journey on this road of life, my life has been filled with testimonies of God's miraculous hand, His direction and guidance, and His voice that has always been and is still speaking with me, daily.

I have always known that there was something significant about my life, and that I am not here by accident. There is a specific purpose for me, and I believe there is for each of us being born into this world. I will not pretend to know the full extent of my purpose here on earth, but I do know I have started on my journey of purpose. One part of my journey is to share, through my testimonies, how good God has been to me, the impact He has had on my life, and how He can do the same for you.

I don't know if it is the same for you, but sometimes when we read the stories of the Bible—illustrations and examples from the Word of God—it is hard to correlate the scriptures to modern-day twentieth-century times. The examples seem so far-fetched. I can only imagine how the average millennial and Generation Z may wonder about the Bible's relevance today.

Although I am not a millennial, nor would I be considered in the Generation Z category, as a youngster, I struggled with the correlation of the scriptures with our modern-day lives. It is through the journey of life and walking daily with the Holy Spirit, the ultimate Teacher, that I have come to recognize that my life, as it plays out, is the same as that of old. I may not be fighting a physical war to defend my faith, although there are men and women in other countries who are, but every decision, trial, and challenge is a warzone in and of itself. My only source of stability is to rely on hearing the voice of God through His Word, daily.

In my modern-day situations, I can hear Him speaking. I hear it in His Word; I hear it when the Holy Spirit reminds me of what I have read in the Word or when He illuminates the Word and causes it to become alive and relevant in my life. I hear His gentle voice guiding me in my choices and making it clear which is the correct path I should take.

In this book, I will share from my own experiences how **God Speaks, Daily** to me. He has impacted my life, and His miraculous fingerprint is in every sphere along the journey. Sometimes we don't hear Him because His voice is so gentle. Sometimes we don't hear Him because there are so many other things clambering for our attention. Sometimes we don't hear Him because we have not been trained to hear Him, and how to recognize His voice, but this does not negate the fact that He is still speaking, even today.

I share from a very practical viewpoint how God speaks. This is an application guide, and it is meant to stir you on to also apply the Word of God in your own life. You are guaranteed to see results. You may just come to the realization that God is speaking and has been speaking to you all along.

So, in our quiet times and in the moments that we take the time to listen, we can re-train ourselves to hear Him speaking, with the able guidance and help of the Holy Spirit, and we will see that **Big Things Happen With the God Who Speaks!**

So, listen up!

Chapter 1
My Son

**My son, do not forget my teaching but
keep my commands in your heart.
(Proverbs 3:1 – AMP).**

My husband and I were teenage sweethearts. It didn't take much at the time to know we were destined to be together. Eight years of courtship culminated in a beautiful wedding when I was twenty-five years old. We had decided that we would be the kind of couple who would enjoy our time of togetherness without the focus on having children early in our marriage. So, we did! We enjoyed private evenings of fine dining; we had the most adventurous time together exploring and finding out more about each other.

In year two of our marriage, we started to imagine life with an addition to our family. By year three, we actively started trying to have our first child, but the timing was not to be. Instead, we were met with nothing—no young ones brewing in the 'oven.' It was then that we knew in our third year of marriage that something was wrong. Our joint visits to our family doctor confirmed what we had been suspecting. The doctor confirmed I had multiple fibroids, which could be a hindrance to us becoming pregnant, but only further tests would confirm whether this was indeed the case. This was the beginning of our uphill battle with infertility and all forms of medical complications.

Over a period of two years, and early in our marriage, we had undertaken almost every fertility test we could have imagined. It was important for both of us to undergo testing together. When we visited our doctor, he started with the obvious questions in relation to our health, lifestyles, and medical histories. There were no significant signs in our assessments, so our doctor decided to go further with his investigations. This was the start of our "rabbit hole" experience, and the testing was extensive, intrusive at times, and exhausting, but we both knew they were necessary to determine the issues we were facing.

The tests were long and drawn out and ranged from the usual pap smear, ovulation tests, numerous blood tests, and urine tests to hormone progesterone checks, regular, scrotal and transvaginal ultrasounds, genetic tests, thyroid tests and procedures to determine if our reproductive organs were functioning correctly. I had to undergo a hysterosalpingogram, otherwise called "tubogram." This is where the doctor injected a liquid dye, and through a series of x-rays, he examined my fallopian tubes and uterus to see whether my fallopian tubes were blocked or if I had defects in my uterus. Between the tests and the many visits to my gynecologist, we were still praying and seeking God's direction. All the test results proved more impossibilities than solutions to our problems.

We were tired and drained, and we sat and listened to the medical expert's findings and pronouncements. Our efforts were not yielding the kind of results our hearts desired, a child. "How could this be? We are young and healthy," was one of the recurring thoughts in my mind. The next two years would be the most significant challenge we would encounter in the early stages of our marriage. It was a difficult period, and it wasn't what either of us anticipated.

He grants the barren woman a home,
Like a joyful mother of children. Praise
the LORD! (Psalm 113:9 – NKJV).

This was my go-to scripture.

God, being the faithful Father He is, sent several persons to encourage and pray with us. Never mind that we had never shared with anyone what we were experiencing at the time. There was one couple the Lord used to minister hope to us in our darkest time of despair.

We had visited another church to attend one of our marriage ministry sessions with the then leaders of the ministry. The session was a success, as it usually was, but little did anyone know that we had been going through a two-year ordeal that felt like it was about to break us. The leaders of the marriage ministry were sensitive to the voice and leadership of the

Holy Spirit that night. They singled us out and began to minister directly to our situation. Up until that point, we had no discussions with anyone about the challenges we were having to get pregnant, and we didn't need to. The Holy Spirit revealed every private detail of our story, and they read us like a book! That night the members of the group held us up in prayer. We left that meeting refreshed with hope that God indeed knew our situation and heard our cries for help.

I had devoted my life so far to always reading the Word of God. I was always fascinated with God's Word, and the pages of the Bible were a playground for my imagination. My relationship with God, and my times spent with Him in devotions, praying and reading, meant everything to me. In the face of many disappointments over the years of trying to get pregnant, endless tears and moments of total frustration, I held on to the thought that "God already knows my situation, and He loves me."

The story of Hannah in 1 Samuel 1 became my story. I read this story countless times to remind myself that if God did it for Hannah, He can certainly do it for me!

My devotions would consist of me spending time with God at the very earliest hours in the morning when I arrived at my office, which was usually before anyone else got in. I would lock myself away in one of the conference rooms, draw the blinds, with my Bible as my only companion. It was during my time of devotion one morning, which was like any other, that I heard the voice of the Lord. He spoke to me from the scriptures in **Proverbs 3:1, "My son, do not forget my teaching but keep my commands in your heart." (AMP).** I had read this verse countless times before, but this time it was different. The words "My son" came alive to me! The verse leapt off the pages. I read it again. Did it just say, "My son?" Somehow, these words became mine. I saw myself in the scriptures. "My son" was referring to my unborn son. Could it be that God was speaking to me about the child to come? I knew what I heard, and I never doubted it for a moment. I chose instead to believe that this was my word. I knew instantly that something different had happened. This word was for me. I held the verse dear to me, and I refused to let it go. I personalized it; I owned it. I knew then that my prayer for a son was answered. God spoke, and I believed.

Daily, I would continue in my time of devotion but with a new excitement and enthusiasm. Although the doctor's visits continued and nothing physically changed that gave us hope, I now had an expectation—I had a word!

That word became alive!

I chose at the time not to tell anyone of my word.

Our attempts to have a child were different from then on for me, all because I believed.

It was a normal day. I took my lunch break and I walked into the cafeteria. I remembered the nauseated feeling that overcame me as I pushed the door of the cafeteria. I knew the smell; I had eaten shepherd's pie so many times before, but this time the odour was different. In that moment, I shared with my closest friend, at the time, the nauseating sensation I encountered. Being a mother of two, she was familiar with the many signs of early pregnancy. That was the day we discovered, in the cubicle of my work restroom, that indeed I was pregnant. Hallelujah! My son had been conceived.

In August 2003, my husband and I celebrated the birth of our first child, a son, named Jevon. He was nineteen years old at the time of writing this book.

A personal word from God will make a demand of you— your faith will be stretched. You must believe your word even when everything around you says otherwise. When you hear God speaking, especially to your intimate situation, trust Him. It may go against the grain, but that is how faith works when it comes alive.

When He speaks, believe Him over everything else!

Chapter 2
One Flesh

**For this reason a man will leave his
father and mother and be united to his
wife, and they will become one flesh.
(Genesis 2:24 – NIV).**

*A*t all times, when I am reading the scriptures, I try to do so with an open mind, ready to receive any new revelations that the Holy Spirit wants to impart. This time was no different.

In January 2020, my husband became ill. We did not know what could have caused it, but the pain was intense and seemed like it was growing daily. This took a toll on our lives. It began firstly with mild pains in the stomach region, then it was more noticeable to his left side, then it escalated and became unbearable. There was the constant presence of pain. The pain seemed to be more severe at night.

One night, after everyone had gone to bed, I had my quiet time praying and reading the Word, as I would normally do. I was reading the book of Genesis, and my focus scripture was Genesis 2:24, **"For this reason a man will leave his father and mother and be united to his wife, and they will become one flesh." (NIV).** This scripture was not unfamiliar to me, as I had read it many times before. On this night, however, I believe the Holy Spirit gave me a personal revelation. He said to me, *"You are one flesh with your husband. This means you can stand in faith with him for his healing. He is frustrated and in pain. You know that Jesus Christ already made provision for his healing; until he experiences a manifestation of healing in his body, you are able to stand with him in faith as if you were seeking to be healed in your own body; he is a part of your body."*

That night, I learnt something of value for my marriage—to intercede for my spouse. His pain was my pain. I was a part of his flesh. I thought it similar to that of a mother giving birth to a child; that child is as much a part of the mother and is literally an extension of her body. We may not think of our spouse being a part of our own flesh because we come from different families and are of no relation. The biblical meaning of "one flesh" speaks to who we have become in the sight of God, and who He intended us as married couples to be. I am indeed bone of his bone and flesh of his flesh, as the Word says, **"And Adam said: "This is now bone of my bones and flesh of my flesh; She shall be called Woman, Because she was taken out of Man." (Genesis 2:23 - NKJV).** We must see and remember who we are in the sight of God.

With a new outlook, probably more of a refresher, I began to pray differently. I prayed as if I was experiencing pain and in need of healing in my own body. I even rejoiced as if healing was granted to me personally. The manifestation of healing in my husband's body took some time, and the process of enduring the sickness and pain was in no way easy, but the light and revelation I got from that word that night gave me the strength I needed to press through the situation. It was my light at the end of the tunnel. I was able to stand with my spouse and encourage him on the journey.

I firmly believe that had it not been for the soothing Word of God, this challenge would have toppled us over as the enemy intended it to.

In your personal quiet times, especially when reading the Word of God, prepare for the Holy Spirit to cause new revelations to come alive. Read with expectation! It is God's desire to have a personal relationship with all His children. Like a good Father, He can use any situation in our lives to minister to us and show Himself strong.

Expect. To. Hear. Him. Speak. Today!

Chapter 3
When Faith Comes

So then faith comes by hearing, and hearing by the word of God. (Romans 10:17 – NKJV).

I tell you the truth, if anyone says to this mountain, Go, throw yourself into the sea and does not doubt in his heart but believes that what he says will happen, it will be done for him. (Mark 11:23 – NIV).

*I*t is amazing when faith comes—when the Word is made flesh. The truth of this word was in the exercise of faith. I had to believe, even when my spouse was in pain and couldn't always believe for himself. Many times, we exist in marriage as individuals trying to be there for each other, but the Lord sees us as one flesh. We could also be in faith as one flesh. We can speak to the mountain as one, we can believe as one, and the result will be done for us as one flesh.

The more I accepted the truth of us being one flesh, the more the Holy Spirit gave us scriptures and truths for us to stand on and not lose hope.

> **He himself bore our sins in his body on the tree, so that we might die to sins and live for righteousness; by His wounds we have been healed. (1 Peter 2:24 – NIV).**

> **No weapon formed against you shall prosper and every tongue that rises in judgment you shall condemn. This is the heritage of the servants of the Lord and this is their vindication from me. (Isaiah 54:17 – KJV).**

> **Surely, he took up our infirmities and carried our sorrow... the punishment that brought us peace was upon him and by his wounds we are healed. (Isaiah 53:4-5 – NIV).**

The scriptures became alive. The Word came to life. Faith came.

> **So then faith comes by hearing, and hearing by the Word of God. (Romans 10:17 –NKJV).**

Although it took time for the manifestation of His healing, the situation seemed less stressful. As we accepted what the Word said to us, the more our faith grew. Faith was now present, so the situation was easier.

"The 'word of the Lord' is designed to reshape your purposes, putting you in a position for Him to do through you what you cannot do on your own." —Priscilla Shirer

Our children knew at the time that something was wrong with their dad, but we didn't know what to tell them. After many visits to the doctor, we were still uncertain what was the cause of all the pain he was experiencing. It was during this time, after months of endurance, that I cried out to God. I went into a time of prayer and fasting where I told the Lord I needed direction and answers. We needed to know what the cause was. My husband was in pain, and doctors could not identify what was the issue.

One night—which in hindsight seemed like the situation was at its worst—the pain was so severe, I felt helpless as I watched him writhe in pain. I laid beside him but there were no words I could speak to comfort him, so I began to declare scriptures of healing. Occasionally, when there would be an ease from the pain, he would nod in agreement. It got so bad and unbearable that I asked him if he wanted me to drive him to the hospital. It was 11 p.m. I felt like I would have taken him wherever he wanted to go. He said yes! So, we got up and dressed and headed out for our one-hour drive. It was almost midnight. All the time, I was praying and declaring that the will of God be done in our lives.

25

When we got to the hospital, we waited for a while to see the doctor, but I was not allowed to go in with him to see the doctor. Afterwards, he was taken to another room to receive a pain injection. I continued to trust God and declare, silently, the will of God be done. When the dust had settled and he emerged from the room, he informed me that the doctor believed he had kidney stones that were probably being expelled from his body. We had to do a few tests to confirm whether the diagnosis was indeed kidney stones, but at least, we finally had an answer to the mysterious illness. We attacked the situation in prayer, calling the culprit by name, "kidney stones." We spoke to the kidney stones in the name of Jesus and commanded that they exit his body and never return.

The victory was in sight, and we kept focused on the promises of God. The tests confirmed it was indeed kidney stones. By then the diagnosis didn't faze us, as we were resolute that complete healing must be manifested. We continued to declare the truth of the Word over every pain. There were sleepless nights, but faith came. We continued to speak the Word even when we saw nothing physically changing. Was it easy? Not at all. In our spirits, we knew we had the victory through Jesus Christ over whatever was insistent on affecting my husband's body and trying to turn our lives upside down. The testimony of the Lord is sure; the kidney stones were many, but God healed him completely, and they are no more. Praise the Lord!

This is the truth, whatever you may be going through today, when faith comes, you will get the supernatural strength and grace you need to carry you through your challenge. Bear in mind though that faith can *only* come through the Word of God. It is God Himself who makes supernatural provisions for His children's faith to grow. His provision is available to you through His Word.

Go ahead and open your Bible today!

Chapter 4
My Daily Bread

Give us this day our daily bread.
(Matthew 6:11 – KJV).

I have always taken the scriptures literally. The Bible represents, to me, real-life situations with real persons. It is filled with experiences, wisdom, examples, and knowledge.

When reading the scriptures, I apply the realness of the Bible's characters to my life.

After my years of high school in Jamaica, I decided to enter the working world. I was focused on funding myself to pursue further studies. I had saved sufficient money to start the first few modules of my tuition. It was a leap of faith, but my way of life was one of faith, and college would prove to be no different. During my years of college, like many other college students, I attended full-time school without much parental support or the comfort of having a job. It was at this time in my life, while at college, that I had learnt how to trust God to take care of my every need. The daily expenses of attending school, finding daily food, transportation costs and any necessary school supplies, were overwhelming. I had to rely on God. He was my source. On a typical day, I would pray and ask God to provide my needs.

In *Matthew 6:10-13*, Jesus taught His disciples how to pray, and this became my daily prayer. Sometimes people may not understand the necessity of such a prayer until they are faced with severe challenges, but this was my go-to prayer as I looked to my heavenly Father for my everyday provisions. The scripture reads:

> **In this manner, therefore, pray: Our Father in heaven, Hallowed be Your name. Your kingdom come. Your will be done on earth as it is in heaven. *Give us this day our daily bread*. And forgive us our debts, as we forgive our debtors. And do not lead us into temptation, but deliver us from the evil one. For Yours is the kingdom and the power and the glory forever. Amen. "For if you forgive men their trespasses, your heavenly Father will also forgive you. But if you do not forgive men their trespasses, neither will your Father forgive your trespasses. (Matthew 6:9-14 – NKJV– emphasis mine).**

I had no choice but to depend on God for my daily bread.

There were many times when there were no funds to even take public transportation to school, but God would supernaturally provide. One day when I had been so desperate, after praying, the thought came to mind to search my closet for any coins. Countless times I would search the clothing hung in my wardrobe to find any money I may have left in my pockets. My searches were rewarded on more than a few occasions with thousands of dollars. *"Did I actually leave thousands of dollars in my pocket?"* I would ask myself. On one occasion, I found JA$10,000. Yes! You read correctly! Without fail, I considered these my personal, everyday miracles. Supernaturally, I would find money in my pockets. I had enough for transportation, food and to share. Isn't God an awesome God!

On other occasions, I would have just enough money to take the transportation to only a part of my journey because I needed to take three different transportations to reach my destination. When I only had sufficient funds for one leg of the journey, I left home in faith! I would be praying all the time while travelling on the first leg of the journey. Under my breath, I would whisper and say, "Lord, You must provide for me. That's what Your Word says." I had occasions where I found money on the roadside. Other times, the Lord would provide "good Samaritans" who offered me rides to my destination. Hallelujah!

I remembered being at a point where I had no money to cover my tuition. This was usually the point when the enemy's voice seemed the loudest in my mind. He was always trying to cause me to doubt that God would come through for me and provide as He promised He would. Granted, sometimes I quickly forgot the miraculous provisions God had done, and I would start to become fretful. I think that is how it must have been for the children of Israel in the wilderness when God performed miracle after miracle, and yet they were forgetful of His provisions.

God is always so faithful! Several times when my tuition was due for payment, and there was no money to pay, I would be contacted by my previous employer and former co-workers to tell me that the company was awarded retroactive money by the government. This happened because I worked in a government job, so when there was an increase in our wages during our time of employment or the government did not pay the increased salaries on time, they would make those payments retroactively. This was indeed miraculous for me as the payments were made in lumpsums, which meant I would have sufficient for tuition. God was my daily provider, and, when He spoke, I took Him at His Word.

Your Daddy (God) wants to bless you with provisions, daily!

Chapter 5
Leave Your Country – Leave Your Home

**The Lord had said to Abram, "Leave
your country, your family and your
father's house and go to the land I will
show you." (Genesis 12:1 – NLV).**

One of the things I have found in my own daily walk
with Jesus Christ is how my daily provisions are made
for me, and can even be found right there in scripture.
Whether there is a financial need, a decision to be made,
clarity needed for the way forward, or instructions, they can
be supplied in scripture.

**And God spoke to Israel in a vision at
night and said "Jacob, Jacob." (Genesis
46:2 – NIV).**

If God knew Jacob's name, He also knows yours. He can
call your name as easily as he called "Jacob, Jacob." God
speaks to us personally, and He can instruct us on what to
do.

The Lord had said to Abram, "Leave your country, your family and your father's house and go to the land I will show you." (Genesis 12:1 – NLV).

Again, He called Abram by name!

We had been married for only a few months and were sharing a home with other family members. It was not the most ideal circumstances as newlyweds, but we made it work. The Lord had impressed on my heart the idea of finding somewhere of our own. As is usually the case, I declared a time of fasting to clearly get direction on whether we would be making the right decision. It was during my time of prayer and seeking the Lord that the scripture in Genesis 12:1 became one of direction on the way forward. It said, **"The Lord had said to Abram, "Leave your country, your family and your father's house and go to the land I will show you." (NLV).** Was this really the Lord's instruction to us to take this path to leave home? After meditating for some time on Genesis 12:1, I was convinced that it was indeed the direction of the Lord.

Nothing says confirmation of an instruction like when things start to fall into place. As soon as I completed my prayer and told the Lord I would trust His leading, a co-worker asked if I knew of someone looking for a house to rent. She was asked to personally recommend someone for the rental property as the owner did not want to advertise the property and open it to random people.

"This seemed too good to be true!" Isn't that sometimes our response, even after knowing we have been praying about a situation for a long time? I think God, in His humour, should slap us upside our heads!

I was in awe. God had literally provided the place for us as it fell into our laps. We met with the landlady and visited the premises. As newlyweds, it was all we could have asked for. At the time, we had no furniture, but we believed if God provided the place, the furniture would have been a little thing for Him to provide as well.

So, we stepped out in faith. The passage had said **"...go to the land I will show you,"** and we trusted that God would show us where He wanted us to go. He did! In the same month, we finalized our agreement for the premises, and we were on our way to living on our own.

This time of living on our own became the building block for our marriage. Like many marriages, we found out that the first few years of living with a spouse, from different backgrounds, with different ideals, meant learning about each other. We trusted God to instruct us, and He did. We could appreciate another phase in our marriage, all because we listened and obeyed when He spoke to us.

God is speaking and instructing you daily through His Word. His Word becomes a beacon to help guide you to make sound and wise choices. The scripture says in **Proverbs 2:9, "Then you will understand what is right, just, and fair, and you will find the right way to go." (NLT).** He

35

encourages us to take paths that are in His will for our lives. Sometimes it may take a leap of faith, but it is worth depending on Him to direct our paths.

Don't you want to know the right way to go? Listen to Him; He will show you!

Chapter 6
He Makes Streams in the Desert

**I tell you the truth Jesus replied, no one
who has left home or brothers or sisters
or mother or father or children or fields
for me and the gospel will fail to receive
a hundred time as much in this present
age (homes, brothers, sisters, mother,
children and fields and with them
persecution) and in the age to come,
eternal life. (Mark 10:29-30 – NIV).**

After we had left our family home, my husband and I
ventured out to live in a rental property on our own.
We got to a point where we desired to own a home.
We didn't have much money, but we had a dream that we
would someday be homeowners. We kept the dream in front
of us by constantly speaking to each other about how we
would become homeowners. The passion and desire began
to swell within us. It was so close that we could see it!

We began to search for scriptures in the Word that spoke
about possessing property. The above Word in Mark 10:29-

30 confirms this. It also says in the scripture, **"Beloved, I pray that you may prosper in all things and be in health, just as your soul prospers." (3 John 1:2 – NKJV).** It is God's desire for us to prosper!

Our faith was built through the spoken word. We even began to put our faith into action as we started saving money for our dream home. A dream can remain untapped if there is no corresponding action. After all, isn't that what faith is all about? We must believe in our hearts, but we must also show that we believe outwardly by taking steps in preparation.

> **"But do you want to know, O foolish man, that faith without works (corresponding action) is dead." (James 2:20 – NKJV- emphasis mine).**

Imagine if the paralytic man and his friends in Mark 2:1-4 remained outside pressing into the crowd like everyone else; that miracle would not have taken place. Instead, they climbed on the roof, opened the roof, and his friends let him down through the roof; these were the corresponding actions to what they desired. What did the Bible say, **"When Jesus saw their faith, he said to the paralytic man, "Son your sins are forgiven you." (Mark 2:5 - NKJV).** Our actions show our faith.

We started looking for properties for sale in the newspapers. We saw some favourable listings too. If the properties were a distance away, we would take a trip to investigate the lands. Granted, this was at a time when we had little savings at the bank, and nothing close to making a deposit on a piece of property let alone making a purchase. Nonetheless, we continued to stand on the truth of the Word.

One day, we stumbled across a piece of property for sale in the newspaper, and we went in search of it. It was in a little quiet community. The area was filled with trees and bushes; there weren't many dwellings at the time. After searching for a while, we finally located the property. It was filled with overgrown bushes and trees, but when we laid eyes on it, we knew it was going to be our land. Without a lot of money, but with a clear vision that this was our dream property, we set our focus on acquiring this land. We stood on scriptures like Proverbs 3:5, **"Trust in the LORD with all your heart and lean not on your own understanding." (NKJV). The** favour of God started to show up in many ways. We had increases and promotions in our jobs; favour at work where we received pro-bono legal support to prepare the documents to purchase the property. We were even able to secure the right funding to facilitate the purchase.

Our focus was on the Word of God, and the provisions were made for us through the Word. Once you have a vision, the vision can far outweigh a situation that is before you. Even if it is a lack of financial resources, our God can provide and make a way when there seems to be no way.

> **Then shall the lame man leap as an**
> **hart, and the tongue of the dumb sing:**
> **for in the wilderness shall waters break**

**out, and streams in the desert." (Isaiah
35:6 – KJV).**

God is looking for believers who will believe! Put some actions to what you are believing for. Today, twenty years later, we are still the owners of this property. God is good; His Word is true, and He is faithful.

Believe what He says; He will do it!

Chapter 7
No Fear of Bad News

Surely, he will never be shaken, a righteous man will be remembered forever. He will have no fear of bad news, his heart is steadfast, trusting in the Lord. (Psalm 112:6-7 – NIV).

*W*hen unexpected and uncontrollable situations shake our lives, God's Word can be the source of our comfort and guide.

In September 2016, I had a *knot in my stomach,* and I knew that something was going to happen. I didn't know what it was, nor did I share this with anyone at the time, but I began to pray and seek the Lord. The sense of uneasiness I felt was almost unbearable. One day, in fasting and prayer, the Holy Spirit impressed Psalm 112 on my heart, and I began to read it. Although I knew the Psalm, I did not know the relevance of it to my situation. I continued in prayer asking the Lord to reveal to me whatever was about to happen.

Again, my peace was found in the scripture in Isaiah 26:3, **"Thou wilt keep him in perfect peace, whose mind is stayed on thee: because he trusteth in thee." (KJV).** This became my spiritual food. I believed what the Word said; God provided perfect peace for me. At the time, I felt a comfort in knowing whatever was to come, it would not surprise God and it couldn't shock Him off His throne.

Less than three weeks later, while at work, I received a telephone call in the mid-morning from my mom. Her voice was not the usual tone, and her first words were "Are you alone? Can you talk?" Instantly, I knew that what I was sensing was about to be revealed. I got up and closed the door to my office and, in that moment, in my heart, I screamed out to God, "Help me!" I composed myself and sat quietly at my desk and said, "Yes, I'm alone. Go ahead. I'm listening." This was to be the beginning of the hardest time in my life.

We discovered that our mother had uterine cancer and immediate treatment was necessary. We went into action. For the next five months, it was a roller coaster ride. It seemed surreal as we watched our mom being whisked into surgery, chemotherapy, and a mound of medical procedures, but God was faithful. His Word kept me in the darkest times and gave me strength I never knew I had.

My brother and I took turns visiting and taking care of her. He went before surgery, and I went after. Before catching the flight to Connecticut, the Holy Spirit guided me to take items for my journey so I could take the Lord's Supper with my mom. I was obedient and packed crackers for the bread, and we used water or juice for the wine.

> **"And when he had given thanks, he break it, and said, Take, eat: this is my body, which is broken for you: this do in remembrance of me. After the same manner also he took the cup, when he had supped, saying, this cup is the new testament in my blood: this do ye, as oft as ye drink it, in remembrance of me."** **(1 Corinthians 11:24-25 – KJV).**

One of the instructions she received from her doctor after surgery was to take an injection in her leg daily. I had the task of administering the injection every afternoon. It was one of the most unpleasant things we had to do, but God had told me to serve communion every day before administering the injection. So, we had supper, read the scripture, prayed, and gave God thanks—every day. What were we doing? We were remembering the Lord's broken body and shed blood every time we had supper. Even in the circumstances, we remembered the provision made for us through Christ Jesus.

I do not pretend to have all the answers; could God have healed my mother? Surely, He could have. As to why she wasn't healed, this much I do know, it was no fault of God's, since His provision of healing was already made for us through His Son over two thousand years ago.

On February 2, 2017, our mom took her final breath. God walked us through the entire process. We were never alone. He saw it coming and, though we didn't know it at the time, this sickness was what took her out of this world and home to be with her Saviour and Lord.

I will end how I began, **"Surely, he will never be shaken, a righteous man will be remembered forever. He will have no fear of bad news, his heart is steadfast, trusting in the Lord." (Psalm 112:6-7 – NIV).**

As for you, child of God, remain focused. Your God is able to take you through *any* circumstance no matter how difficult it may seem!

Chapter 8
The Year of the Bible

My son, pay attention to what I say, listen closely to my words. Do not let them out of your sight, keep them within your heart; for they are life to those who find them and health to a man's whole body. (Proverbs 4:20-22 – NIV).

*T*he year 2020 was declared as *"The Year of the Bible."* That year I decided that in every situation, decision, challenge, and issue that I would face, I would build a foundation on the Word, and I would move in accordance with whatever the Word of God said.

"He also said, "This is what the kingdom of God is like. A man scatters seed on the ground. Night and day, whether he sleeps or gets up, the seed sprouts and grows, though he does not know how. All by itself the soil produces grain – the stalk, then the head, then the

**full kernel in the head." (Mark 4:26-28
– NIV).**

Armed with the scripture in Mark 4:26-28, I set out to scatter the seed of God's Word on the *ground*. I would scatter the Word every day. I would sleep and rise, believe and declare that whatever the scripture said is true, and it will come to pass. Whatever it is that I was believing God for, the miracle of the Word would work to cause it to sprout and grow. All by itself, the Word must produce, and all it required was that I speak it to scatter the seed. The Word must work! Do not be deterred; do not be sidetracked; do not be distracted! Continue to sow the Word because the soil must yield!

> **My son, pay attention to what I say,
> listen closely to my words. Do not let
> them out of your sight, keep them
> within your heart; for they are life to
> those who find them and health to a
> man's whole body. (Proverbs 4:20-22 –
> NIV).**

I purposed not to listen to the negative words of *others*, whether those were the words of the media, social media, friends or even family. If their words did not align with the Word of God, then I would not *"keep them in my heart."* I gave myself permission to remove any word that was spoken that, in my opinion, did not line up with God's Word.

If the Word of God, once found, brings life and health to a man's whole body, then my expectation was *only* life and health!

> **I pray also that the eyes of your heart**
> **may be enlightened in order that you**
> **may know the hope to which he has**
> **called you, the riches of his glorious**
> **inheritance in the saints and his**
> **incomparably great power for us who**
> **believe. (Ephesians 1:18-19 – NIV).**

In February 2020, I was impressed to pray and ask God's direction, and His instruction as to what His purpose for my life was. I believe there is a specific purpose that God has for each of us. He said in Psalms 139:16 that, **"...All the days ordained for me were written in your book before one of them came to be." (NIV).** He established, spoke, and wrote down His purpose for your life. Don't you want to know what that purpose is? I wanted to know, and He was faithful enough to reveal it to me.

Some people may think you are presumptuous to ask God to make plain His purpose for you, but the Bible says, **"Where there is no vision, the people perish: but he that keepeth the law, happy is he." (Proverbs 29:18 - KJV).** Therefore, with a vision, the people prosper! I prefer to have a vision and prosper in all I do, rather than living life aimlessly.

You can ask God today to make His vision and purpose for your life plain.

Chapter 9
Where Do You Live?

He who dwells in the shelter of the Most High will rest in the shadow of the Almighty. I will say of the Lord, "He is my refuge and my fortress, my God in whom I trust." (Psalm 91:1-2 – NIV).

The onset of the COVID-19 pandemic had reached the shores of Jamaica. While there were so many speculations and rumors in December 2019 of the virus being present in Jamaica, by March 2020, it was obvious that the virus was on the island and growing in numbers. The concerns and fears were also growing with the number of cases. The news carried on the local and international media aided with growing the fears of everyone. People were ingesting a daily dose of the news as they watched the number of cases climb. There were some who were unaffected, but for many people it seemed that an epidemic, like we have never seen before in our generation, had come home. The virus became the conversation on the lips of everyone, in every circle of life.

On March 4, 2020, the Word of God in Psalm 91 became my food. I found it; I ate it. I declared this Word over my life and that of my family:

> **He who dwells in the shelter of the Most High will rest in the shadow of the Almighty. I will say of the Lord, "He is my refuge and my fortress, my God in whom I trust." (Psalm 91:1-2 – NIV).**

These were my notes from the scripture:

1. We dwell in a place of safety.
2. We dwell in a place of faith.
3. This is our default position.
4. We dwell in this shelter permanently; we are not visiting.

I am certain that what was happening in Jamaica was also happening elsewhere in the world. In the early stages of the virus, those who had caught it were often ostracized. We saw an unpleasant side of our countrymen. Families had turned against families, neighbours against neighbours, and workplaces were being driven by decisions that were rooted in fear. It was all around us, and some people were being compelled to take vaccinations without understanding the full implications on their own bodies.

In August 2021, the Word that God spoke to my family came from **Psalm 29:11, "The LORD will give strength to His people; The LORD will bless His people with peace."**

(NIV). Our focus became who God said we were; people with strength and peace.

Although we live in a world full of sicknesses, darkness, and corruption, there is always light and life for those who want it. God is a giving God. In place of our weakness and lack, God gives us strength. Amidst the turmoil around us, God gives us peace. These gifts and provisions of God are spiritually discerned, that is, we are equipped in our re-created spirit. They are not dependent on our outward circumstances. His peace can sustain us regardless of what is going on around us. His strength propels His people to victory, while others may seem to be falling.

We can abide in His presence through the Word, and as we fellowship daily with Him. There is a spiritual reservoir of life that is available to us, if we choose to dwell in His shelter.

We have strength; we are strength-equipped!

We have peace; we are peace-equipped!

These are some other scriptures that the Holy Spirit led me to:

> **In righteousness you will be established.**
> **Oppression or tyranny will be far from**
> **you, you will have nothing to fear.**
> **Terror will be far removed; it will not**
> **come near you. (Isaiah 54:14 – NIV).**

**Peace I leave with you; my peace I give
you. I do not give to you as the world
gives. Do not let your hearts be troubled
and do not be afraid. (John 14:27 –
NIV).**

**I have told you these things, so that in
me you may have peace. In this world
you will have trouble but take heart. I
have overcome the world. (John 16:33 –
NIV).**

In times of fear, as the people of God, we must remember
that the Word is what God wants us to use as our weapon.
Whenever fear arises, we must speak the Word to magnify
the truth of God above the fear. Otherwise, the people of God
will tremble and become as terrified as those of the world.
These scriptures became *"life to our whole body"* at a time
when the world seemed to have been going through a
midnight hour. God was faithful, and He kept us safely.

We decided, at the time, as a family, not to discuss any
precautions or measures we would take with others in
relation to COVID-19. Our decisions were ours to make, and
we would be guided by the Word of God and the peace of
the Holy Spirit.

We also took the opportunity to teach our children a valuable
lesson, to not be affected or guided by the decisions of the
masses. Make your decisions based on your assessment of a
situation, the Word of God, and the peace of God in your

own lives. None of us had ever before encountered a pandemic of this nature, and it was a learning opportunity for us all.

My heart goes out to you or your family who may have been affected by COVID-19 in some way. Whether you suffered the loss of loved ones, or were seriously impacted by the virus, we are reminded that we are not exempt from what goes on around us, but we have the comfort that, **"Peace I leave with you, my peace I give to you; not as the world gives do I give to you. Let not your heart be troubled, neither let it be afraid." (John 14:27 – NIV).**

God is still speaking words of peace to you today as He did in the days of old.

Chapter 10
He Overcame the World

These things I have spoken to you, that in Me you may have peace. In the world you will have tribulation; but be of good cheer, I have overcome the world. (John 16:33 – NIV).

Second to 2017, 2020 was one of the most challenging years of my life. I dubbed it the "Year of Faith and Endurance."

There were so many challenges in this year that caused me to make some life-changing decisions. These were the kinds of "sink or swim" decisions that if God didn't come through for me, it could be disastrous. I had to put my trust in Him. He had directed me to move on from the comfort of a job I had been at for over ten years. It was reliable, predictable, and I had a fixed salary. This meant I had to walk out on a limb. While the decision was not without its fair share of mishaps, it was the words in John 16:33 that added direction and peace to my life:

**"These things I have spoken to you,
that in Me you may have peace. In the
world you will have tribulation; but be
of good cheer, I have overcome the
world." (NIV).**

Again, this is a scripture I had read on many occasions, but I now recognized the command in this verse to *"be of good cheer."* In other words, not just merriment, optimism, and good spirits, but the word "good" before the word "cheer" suggests that we should have *excellent cheer.* This means you should be over-the-top optimistic because you are certain that Jesus overcame and gave you the victory in whatever situation you are faced with. That, for me, was great news.

It is never easy when you face situations of lies, hypocrisy, disappointments, and betrayal, to remember to be of good cheer. Through it all, the Word of God spoke to me daily, guiding me.

I can only imagine what David endured in 1 Samuel 30. He had a major conflict on his hands with the Amalekites. The Amalekites had invaded his city; attacked and burnt it; taken the women and children captives while he and his men were away and unable to defend them. To make matters worse, his two wives were also taken captive. Through it all, his own men were thinking of stoning him to death, but the Word said in 1 Samuel 30:6, **"...But David found strength *(encouraged himself)* in the Lord." (NIV – emphasis mine).**

Sometimes when there is no other source of encouragement, you must learn to encourage yourself. This is what I did! With all the changes that were happening, my mind tried to play tricks on me that God wasn't with me. I had to speak words of encouragement to my soul.

If people were to hear some of us in times like these, they would think we are mad and out of our minds. Encouragement sometimes means speaking to yourself and affirming who God says you are. Other people would want to pronounce their version of who they think you are or who you appear to be, but you must learn to stand securely on who the Word of God says you are. Otherwise, not only will Satan speak words of condemnation over you, but he will try to infiltrate your mind, and some people may even begin to believe his lies.

Remember what the Word says in **Proverbs 18:21, "Death and life are in the power of the tongue, and those who love it will eat its fruit." (NKJV).** It also says in **Job 22:28, "You will also declare a thing, and it will be established for you; So light will shine on your ways." (NKJV).** It is necessary that *you* declare. *You* must speak and affirm the Word of God. *You* must agree with what He says about you. No one else can do that for you.

During this time, the Word of God was loud in my ear:

> **I say to you, my friends, do not be**
> **afraid of those who kill the body and**

> **after that have nothing more that they can do. (Luke 12:4 – NKJV).**

> **Then He said to His disciples, "Therefore I say to you, do not worry about your life, what you will eat; nor about the body, what you will put on." (Luke 12:22 – NKJV).**

> **For He is our God. We are the people he watches over, the flock under his care. (Psalm 95:7 – NKJV).**

In order for the Word to be magnified above the situations you face, you must open your mouth and speak to them.

At a time when everything seemed to have been against me—the uncertainty of my situation—I didn't know what to do. God spoke to me through His Word, and I magnified His Word above everything else.

You can do the same! Magnify God's Word above your own situations.

Chapter 11
Don't Flinch!

**He replied, "The knowledge of the
secrets of the kingdom of heaven has
been given to you, but not to
them." (Matthew 13:11 – NIV).**

I was home on September 7, 2020, seeking the Lord and
praying about the various issues that were going on in
my life. After spending the entire day meditating on
Matthew 13, which speaks primarily of the kingdom of
heaven, I laid quietly across my bed. I heard the Holy Spirit's
voice say to me "Don't flinch." I was certain it was Him
speaking because the words were outside of anything I was
even thinking about. I instantly got up thinking to myself,
"What does that even mean?" I searched for the meaning of
the word "flinch."

*Flinch means: to make a quick, nervous movement as an
instinctive reaction to fear, pain or surprise.*

Though armed with the definition of the word, I had more
questions than answers. What was happening that I was

making a quick, nervous movement about as a reaction to fear, pain or surprise in my life? I began to pray. I rested in the thought that the Holy Spirit, who is my Teacher, **"will tell me what is yet to come."** (see John 16:13).

Over the years, I would adopt this instruction. I would often remind myself not to make any quick, nervous movement in reaction to fear, pain or surprise. With this, I also assessed my situations differently, to ensure I tried to be obedient to His instruction.

I speak to you as He did to me, child of God, "Don't flinch!"

Chapter 12
Keep Looking at Jesus!

"…and let us run with perseverance the race marked out for us. Let us fix our eyes on Jesus, the author and perfector of our faith." (Hebrews 12:1b – NIV).

Each of us has been assigned a race to run; that is my belief. Sometimes, however, we focus on how someone else is running their race and we get sidetracked. We even begin to run a race that was not meant for us.

For two years, my husband and I felt impressed that the Lord was calling us to do more in ministry. We knew that we heard His voice, but we did not receive any further instructions. So, we patiently waited for His lead.

It wasn't until June 2021 that we understood that we were being called to relocate to another church to assist with kingdom building. Hebrews 12:1 was where we found direction and answers on how to execute our transition. The more we meditated on this Word, the more we appreciated that there is a race that is marked out for us to run. It was time to run another leg of the race God had assigned for us. The situation around us did not, at the time, support us moving in this direction. After all, we had been members of our church for over twenty years. We had served in various leadership roles; our children were born into this congregation; up to that point in our lives, every significant thing that had happened to us was surrounded by the friends and support of our church. How could God be telling us it was time to go?

Sometimes the thought of leaving a comfortable environment can cripple you and delay your move. It was a major decision for us, and we wanted to be certain we were hearing from God. One morning in prayer, I heard the Lord say, "It's time to relocate to another part of the vineyard." I had never thought of our move like that, but I understood what He was calling us to do. We would not be leaving the vineyard, which represents the body of Christ; we were simply being called to assist in another area of the vineyard that needed our help to grow in the Word. We were excited! Direction and clarity had come through the very Word of God.

We notified the leaders of our church at the time. God provided favour and support in our departure. Our pastor released us with his blessings, and we were most grateful.

The Lord caused us to find roots in a ministry that was just starting out. Fingers from the Heart Ministries had been so impactful in touching the lives of many people all over the world during the lockdown of the COVID-19 pandemic. Many new converts were coming into the kingdom, and many people had recommitted their lives to Jesus Christ. It was therefore necessary for them to have someone to teach them the Word. We dived right into ministry and began to teach the Word with the help of the Holy Spirit.

Your greatest work is for you to acknowledge that the call of God is on your life, and you can share with others the love of God and the saving grace of His Son, Jesus Christ. Everything you do should be propelled by the need to run your race for Jesus Christ. Others will know and experience God, even if that means you should relocate or adjust your plans for the greater call of God.

Maybe you are in such a position where the Holy Spirit has impressed it on your heart to go into ministry, but nothing around you supports such a decision. You may be fearful to take the first step, wondering if you really heard from God. God will provide the clarity you need for where He has called you to be.

"No matter what has happened to you in the past or what is going on in your life right now, it has no power to keep you from having an amazingly good future if you will walk by faith in God. God loves you! He wants you to live with victory over sin so you can possess His promises for your life today." —Joyce Meyer

Chapter 13
A Glimpse of the Puzzle: Why Am I Here?

This is because Ezra had determined to study and obey the law of the Lord and to teach those decrees and regulations to the people of Israel. (Ezra 7:10 – NLT).

*W*hen your purpose is revealed, you begin to live your life with meaning.

When there is no purpose, it is like being handed hundreds of small puzzle pieces for you to complete the puzzle, without you even knowing what the completed puzzle looks like. As for me, I was determined not to journey any further in my life without having a glimpse of what was the puzzle picture. I wanted instructions, so I spent a period in prayer and reading the Word for direction.

On April 15, 2021, armed with **Proverbs 20:5, "the purpose in a man's heart is like deep water, but a man of understanding will draw it out" (NIV),** I began to ask questions of the Lord as to His purpose for my life. I was determined to understand my purpose, and I would draw out any wisdom I needed. I was led to the book of Ezra, which I diligently read. When reading, I got to **Ezra 7:10, "For Ezra had prepared his heart to seek the Law of the Lord, and to do it, and to teach statutes and ordinances in Israel." (NLT).**

This verse came alive for me. The Holy Spirit used this verse to show me my purpose. That is when I heard, "This is you!" Finally, I was given a glimpse of my finished puzzle. "This is me," I repeated to myself. I accepted this as my truth. I am called to be a teacher in the house of the Lord.

I realized then that when the Word speaks truth to us, that is, *"walking by faith and not by sight,"* it is a personal decision for you to either believe it or not. You can either believe the Word as the truth or reject it. I chose to believe who the Lord said I am, and my entire life changed from that moment on.

Are you satisfied with the pieces of your puzzle, or do you want to know who you are called to be in the body of Christ? Simply ask. It is God's desire to guide you in the path that He wants you to take.

Chapter 14
I Am God's Masterpiece!

**For we are God's masterpiece. He has
created us anew in Christ Jesus, so we
can do the good things he planned for us
long ago. (Ephesians 2:10 – NLT).**

*I*t is not every day that you will feel like a conqueror, and that is okay. It is at those times we must remember that our Christian journey is not limited to, nor is it made up of how we feel. We are who God says we are. As Joyce Meyer said, "Do not give your feeling a vote." We are conquerors because of the finished works of Jesus Christ.

It is on the monotonous ground hog days—the ones that involve cooking, or doing daily chores; going to the grocery store; traffic; picking up and dropping off the kids from school; dealing with a sick child all night with fever, and the fever probably broke at 4 a.m., feeling defeated and useless, with the last ounce of energy gone—that you remind yourself of who God says you are. You are His masterpiece! "As monotonous as the day may be, I am God's masterpiece!"

Sometimes it is hard to identify God's purpose in a routine day. When our children were younger, I remember teaching them how to pray; teaching them a Bible verse or just sitting and talking with them about various things, when they felt like it. I realized then that that may have been my greatest ministry—teaching and training my children in the way they should go, so that when they are old, they will not depart from it – **"Train up a child in the way he should go: and when he is old, he will not depart from it." (Proverbs 22:6 - KJV).**

So, whoever you are, as you read through the pages of this book, remember who you are. You are God's masterpiece, created in Christ to do good works which He planned for you long ago *(see Ephesians 2:10)*.

You can do this!

Chapter 15
Believe!

And all this, whatsoever you shall ask in prayer, believing, you shall receive. (Matthew 21:22 – AMP).

*M*y brother and his family were actively preparing for their life-changing move to another state because of his promotion. The housing situation had changed in recent years, and there was a frantic bidding war for any reasonable livable space. Their move was no different. They needed a home, and nothing was on the market. The time was ticking, and the moving date had been arranged, but there was no house.

To aid their realtor and to speed the process along, he and his wife journeyed out of state in search of a suitable home. The search was tiresome, and the pickings were not suitable. There was one place, however, that was beautiful but outside of their budget. His wife was even furious with the realtor and asked, "Why would you carry us to see something like this, knowing full well we cannot afford it?"

That night, my telephone rang at 10 p.m. It was my sister-in-law. While she updated me on the day's activities, you could hear the frustration in her voice. She confessed how hopeless the housing market seemed to be. During our conversation, there was a glimmer of excitement as she talked about the house that was outside of their budget. She said she couldn't get it out of her mind, but she knew it was out of their price range.

We know there is nothing that is too hard for God. I asked her if she wanted the house. She said, "Yes!"

"Well then," I said, "Let's stand on the scripture; **and all this, whatsoever you shall ask in prayer, believing, you shall receive." (Matthew 21:22 – AMP).** We prayed; we agreed with what the word said, and we declared that this was our "Whatsoever" case that we were bringing to God. We invited God's possibilities to show up in their circumstances, and we asked Him to bring to pass what seemed impossible.

They made their offer and went home. Like any other housing situation, a bidding war ensued, but God's favour was upon them. Their offer was successful, and what seemed impossible, out of reach, too expensive, was now theirs. Only God could have worked it out. We stood on the Word, and God worked out our "Whatsoever" case.

So, I say to you, whatsoever you shall ask in prayer, believe!

Chapter 16
The Word of God is the Final Authority in My Life

Blessed [fortunate, prosperous, and favored by God] is the man who does not walk in the counsel of the wicked [following their advice and example], nor stand in the path of sinners, nor sit [down to rest] in the seat of scoffers (ridiculers). But his delight is in the law of the LORD, and on His law [His precepts and teachings] he [habitually] meditates [ponders and studies] day and night. And he will be like a tree firmly planted [and fed] by streams of water, which yields its fruit in its season; Its leaf does not wither; and in whatever he does, he prospers [and comes to maturity]. The wicked [those who live in disobedience to God's law] are not so, but they are like the chaff [worthless and without substance] which the wind

**blows away. Therefore the wicked will
not stand [unpunished] in the judgment,
Nor sinners in the assembly of the
righteous. For the LORD knows and
fully approves the way of the righteous,
but the way of the wicked shall perish.
(Psalm 1:1-6 – AMP).**

Do you have a go-to scripture? Psalm 1 is my go-to chapter.

On January 7, 2018, I decided that no matter how busy I was, I would find time to declare this scripture out loud every day. I wrote the full passage from the version I wanted in the back of my Bible. I would pace the floor of my room while declaring this passage. I personalized it and at the ending I said, "the Word of the Lord is the final authority in my life!"

I have seen this scripture come alive in my life.

What is your go-to Word that God wants you to agree and speak daily over your life?

Chapter 17
My Encounter

**But Jesus called them to Him and said,
"Let the little children come to Me, and
do not forbid them; for of such is the
kingdom of God." (Luke 18:16 – NKJV).**

*M*y mother started attending church when we were
toddlers. She did not commit her life to Jesus
Christ until I was about six years old. My brother
and I (my sister was still a baby) were not popular kids, but
we were known as the children who were always at church.
My mother made certain of that.

Our mom, like most parents in Jamaica, insisted that we
attend Sunday School and Children's Church. This was
never an option for us, nor was it up for debate. It was in
Sunday School and Children's Church that we were taught
the stories of the Bible. The characters and adventures in the
Bible became real to life. There was no limit to our
imagination. We were taught to pray, to be kind, to be gentle,
to look after each other, and to show love in all we did. This
was the beginning of a journey of great adventures.

Somewhere in the stories of the Bible characters and the teachings by some of the best young ministers, I heard about Jesus and His love for me, and I believed.

Our classes were brimming over in the packed room filled with children, some eager to learn, others up to pure mischief. Somewhere, in what seemed to have been the routine of Sunday School, I had an encounter with Jesus Christ. It intrigued me how someone I barely knew before I was even born, loved me. I was introduced to who Jesus is, and what He did for me, through the many stories I heard, but it was when I believed that I finally understood how much He truly loved me.

When you encounter the Son of God, Jesus Christ, you are willing to leave your way of life, if needs be, leave your occupation—as the fishermen did. Your eyes can be opened to see what you couldn't see for forty years. Your body, though crippled, gets up and all the faculties start to function as they should. You forget that you were on your way for water; instead, you run into the town and village to declare **"Come see a man." (John 4:29 - KJV).** An encounter with Jesus Christ is all it takes to change the trajectory of your life. When you encounter Christ, your ministry and purpose for living become clearer.

"Ministry is when the people who hear you, don't want more of you; they want more of Him because of what you've said. When you point them to God's fire instead of trying to get attention for yourself, that's ministry." —Priscilla Shirer

After giving my life to Jesus, at that tender age, the next step seemed to be baptism, which at my age looked like people being dunked under the water after confessing their faith. One Sunday, it was announced that there would be a baptismal service to be held that evening. Anyone who was interested in being baptized was instructed to be prepared to do so that evening.

We went home after church that Sunday and told our mother of our intention to be baptized. My mom, in her usual way, said to us, "If you need a bath, go and fill the tub and you and your brother can get in." That was her way of cautioning us on the course of action we were planning to take. Do not get me wrong, my mother loved us and wanted nothing more than to see us come to Christ, but she also knew that this decision would change our lives forever.

I made my decision that evening. I wanted to take the next step after believing and accepting Jesus. I found my clothing and packed my bag. The time could not pass quickly enough. We were excited. I heard my mom's caution, but I also knew there was something more urgent in my heart. I had encountered Jesus and His love, and now there was no turning back. I began to love the person I knew loved me. With my few clothing items in hand, I secretly left home and headed off to church, which was within walking distance from my home. My brother soon joined me, and, soon after, my mother was among the crowd of witnesses gathered to see her two young children baptized in water.

That Sunday evening, under the confession of our faith, we were baptized. My encounter with Jesus Christ at that age led to a lifetime journey. He constantly reveals His love for me every step of the journey.

> **And I, if I be lifted up from the earth,**
> **will draw all men unto me." (John 12:32**
> **– KJV).**

If you have not encountered Jesus Christ before, you can do so today.

> **"That if you confess with your mouth**
> **the Lord Jesus and believe in your heart**
> **that God has raised Him from the dead,**
> **you will be saved." (Romans 10:9 –**
> **NKJV).**

Chapter 18
He Had an Encounter with Christ

And they said to one another, "Did not our heart burn within us while He talked with us on the road, and while He opened the Scriptures to us?" (Luke 24:32 – NKJV).

We had been journeying to the major towns around Jamaica to read the Word of God. It was a vision of Pastor Phillip Johnson of the Solid Base Foundation that had come alive. He led a team of volunteers who made it their mandate to read the Bible from Genesis to Revelation to anyone who would listen. We discovered that it would take us six days to read the entire Bible from 6 a.m. to 10 p.m. each day in one location. It is called the Bible Marathon.

On a Sunday afternoon, we would pitch our huge tent and prepare seating for our guests who would come by daily to hear or participate in the reading of the Bible. This was no ordinary street meeting; it was a time to hear the undiluted Word of God. It was not a worship service; we had no praise and worship session, as the focus was to read the Word so that men could hear God speak through His Word to their hearts. There was something about hearing the undiluted Word of God!

People in the town would sometimes be apprehensive toward us, not understanding why we did what we did; enquiring eyes from school children as they waited close by to wait on their buses, or curious street vendors who would realize within a day or two that we were blessing their hometown by simply reading from the Word of God. The reception was overwhelming, and men and women encountered and heard the voice of God in a profound way.

Like any other morning, we started reading as people busily went about their business. The tent was fairly empty, as it usually is at 6 a.m., except for the team members who were present to read. The coconut man was on spot, and the supermarket was just about to open its doors. We could hear the playing of music in the distance, which was commonplace for weekend music sessions in Jamaica. While I was reading, a few ladies stopped by the tent seemingly coming from their night festivities. They were a welcome sight, and they lingered a while to hear the reading of the Word.

At the end of my reading session, I went to stand at the front of the tent. The passersby would greet us with a "Good morning," and some would nod in approval as if saying "Keep up the good work." It was then that I noticed a young man walking towards the front of the tent. He was clad in his party outfit as if coming in from a night of festivities. As he leaned on one of the stakes of the tent, I said to him, "Good morning," and I made small talk. He shared that he was at a bar a block away drinking and winding down to go home when he heard our reading in the distance. Curious, he made his way to the tent. He listened in silence for a long time and, as if recognizing that there was no need to fear, he began speaking. We spoke for nearly two hours as the man poured out his life to me. He confessed his lifestyle and told me about the gang he was a part of. He seemed to have been well-known. Several times he asked if I knew who he was. I didn't. It was noticeable that everyone else around knew exactly who he was, as people would stare, and many would "hail" him as they passed by. He was famous. Whether in a good way or bad, I didn't know at the time. After hearing his many stories, I had to surmise that indeed I was speaking with an infamous killer or, as they would be called in Jamaica, a "gunman."

The stories he shared should have made me quiver in fear, but they didn't. Instead, I saw a lost soul who needed to hear the message of salvation and Jesus' love for him. I listened as he continued to share, and the more he did, the more he seemed to be compelled to declare the truth of his lifestyle.

Never had I come face to face with such a cold-blooded person. His smile and warm conversation made me realize that this man was telling me about the man behind the man. I listened while praying silently, asking God to tell me what to say and how to minister His truth to this man. When he was finished speaking, and it seemed like he had confessed everything without restriction, he went silent. This was my moment. I began to share with him about a man named Saul and his encounter with Jesus. I could see the interest in his eyes. This man also had an encounter with Jesus Christ at the tent that morning. He said he felt as if he was unable to move away. Several times in the conversation he pleaded, "Why are you guys here?" as if unable to comprehend the conviction he felt and the arrest his soul was under. We bonded that day, and I told him about Jesus Christ. I told him only Jesus could make a change in his life.

He was convinced that he couldn't change as he was too lost. He thought no one would forgive someone like him if they knew the gruesome things he had done. He was concerned that those around him who saw him as a leader would not only think he had become weak, but they wouldn't understand him laying down his weapons. I told him "Jesus Christ already forgave you and there's nothing you can do about it." I had to devise a plan. I silently asked the Holy Spirit to tell me what to say. I was instructed to say, "When you get home, tonight, when no one else is around, find somewhere quiet, even in the bathroom, pray and ask the Lord to come into your heart." He nodded. He said nothing further, but the plan seemed to have put his mind at peace. He left.

I wish I could tell you the outcome and what happened to my "friend," whether he followed through with our plan or not, but I cannot. We parted that day and I never heard from him, nor do I know what happened to him. I only know I met a young man who had an encounter with Jesus Christ that day. My prayer is that God, in His mercy, heard his heart, and that the Holy Spirit, who led him to our tent, would also minister to him so he surrenders his life to Jesus Christ.

We are called to minister the love of God to a lost and dying world.

Chapter 19
An Incident at the Airport

God is in the midst of her, she shall not be moved; God shall help her, just at the break of dawn. (Psalm 46:5 – NKJV).

In August 2021, I had been meditating on the scripture in Deuteronomy 2:7a, which states, **"For the LORD your God has blessed you in all the work of your hand." (NKJV).** This had been my daily declaration.

One day, while driving home from work, a friend called. It had been a while since we spoke, so I was delighted to hear from her. She said, "How long has it been since you last saw your brother? Don't you want to take a trip to see him?" Of course, she was aware that my brother lived in America, but she didn't know he had recently relocated to another state with his family.

For some time, my brother's wife kept insisting "When are you going to take a trip to come and see this miraculous house that we prayed into existence?" The Lord knew that this was one of my heart's desires, but it was not among my things to do. God indeed **"Gives you the desires of our**

heart." (Psalm 37:4 - NKJV). My friend gifted me that day with a paid airline ticket to any destination of my choice. Most certainly, my trip would be to my sister-in-law's new home. *"Was this a prank? She wouldn't dare prank me like this?"* I kept saying to myself. Could it be that God was kind enough to use someone to gift me the very desire of my heart? God really likes me!

As simple as a trip may seem, I water my steps in prayer. Whatever I do, wherever I go, I recognize that in my movements, whether I walk, drive or fly, it is an opportunity to carry the glory of God with me. At any time, we should be available to be used to effect change in any circumstance around us.

"I resolved to stop using physical means to fight battles that require spiritual remedies, using instead the power of prayer to do what it's always been designed to do." —Priscilla Shirer

It was the day of my trip, and I was fully packed and ready to go. As usual, I prayed and asked God's guidance on the trip, and for His perfect will to be done in every area of my life, including my travel plans.

My flight was a connecting flight through JFK International Airport to Buffalo, New York. I had arrived at my destination at JFK, and my first intention was to find a Dunkin' Donuts shop to get my old-fashioned donuts and a cup of coffee. With my prize donuts and coffee in hand, I scoured the airport to find a quiet location away from the crowd to sit and satisfy my craving. As I made my way towards a row of seats closest to the window, I noticed that there was a lady and her son seated five chairs away. "That's not bad," I thought. "It's just two of them; there's no crowd." So, I sat down. As soon as I sat down, I saw another family member heading towards them. Sure enough, there were two additional family members who had gone to buy food. My donut was tasty, and my coffee hit the spot, so I didn't care anymore whether others came.

In that moment, without fully understanding why, I felt as if something was wrong, so I whispered a prayer. Less than five seconds later, I saw the girl from the corner of my eye, one of the family members, pounding at her chest. The girl was choking, and the mother and other family members went into panic mode. As soon as people recognized what was happening, the screaming intensified. Passersby were helplessly making frantic gestures. The young lady, helpless to cough whatever was lodged in her throat, fainted. Her mother and siblings were hysterical. It was pandemonium. In between the screams for help and calling the paramedic, I was able to pray, "Father, in the name of Jesus Christ, I speak life over this girl. She shall not die! Whatever is causing this issue, I pray that the object be dislodged and come out of her throat now, in Jesus' name. I speak life; there will be no death in this airport today." In what seemed like an incredible act of courage, the mother, as if remembering that she knew what to do and realizing that her child was choking, immediately started the Heimlich maneuver. By the third pumping to her daughter's chest, the object flew out. It was a piece of chicken nugget that had lodged in the child's throat, and she was unable to breathe.

The police officers and paramedics would not have reached the girl in time if the mother had not sprung into action. Help came, and not before long, the area was swarmed with police officers and paramedics. But, by then, we all witnessed the miraculous saving of a child's life.

I do not know what would have happened, had her mother not regained herself and tried to save her child's life. I believe that situation could have gone terribly wrong that day, and we could have been staring at a dead child on the carpet. It is in moments like these that a child of God can hear the voice of God and move into action. Whether that action means whispering a prayer or declaring life in a situation where it could have been death or speaking peace in the middle of turmoil, if praying is what you can do, then do it. There is power in prayer!

> **My sheep hear My voice, and I know them, and they follow Me. (John 10:27 – KJV).**

Wherever you are, whatever is happening around you, listening for the voice of God and His guidance could mean an answer, deliverance, direction or even a miracle in the moment. This incident could have happened anywhere in this airport—it is a big place—but it happened exactly where I was seated, five chairs down; the same section; the same row.

A mere coincidence, you may say. I think not!

Chapter 20
As He Is, So Am I In This World!

**The centurion answered and said,
"Lord, I am not worthy that You should
come under my roof. But only speak a
word, and my servant will be healed."
When Jesus heard it, He marveled, and
said to those who followed, "Assuredly, I
say to you, I have not found such great
faith, not even in Israel!" Then Jesus
said to the centurion, "Go your way;
and as you have believed, so let it be
done for you." And his servant was
healed that same hour. (Matthew
8:8,10,13 – NKJV).**

Sometimes you read scriptures like this example of the
centurion, and you cannot help but compare yourself
with the centurion's faith. If some of us were to be
brutally honest, which I usually am, we would say our faith
is woefully lacking in comparison to that of the centurion's.

I thought of how great the centurion's faith was that even Jesus praised him for his great faith. I wanted great faith like that—to believe for something and to see it come to pass.

While I was driving home from work one day, another scripture popped into my head. It was **1 John 4:17, "Love has been perfected among us in this: that we may have boldness in the day of judgment; *because as He is, so are we in this world.*" (NKJV - emphasis mine).**

It was then that the Holy Spirit pointed out, *"As He is, so are you in this world. Do you understand that you can have whatever you want?"* I immediately understood! Instead of aiming for the centurion's faith, I had to recognize who I have on the inside of me. Jesus Christ, the Saviour and Son of God, lives on the inside of me. The centurion's faith was admirable; after all, Christ commended him for it, but let's focus on Jesus for a moment. Jesus had faith in His Father. His faith was even greater than that of the centurion's. He knew the power that was inside Him because God was with Him, and He was about His Father's business. Knowing this, which faith would you want? That of the centurion or that of Jesus?

"As Jesus is, so am I in this world!"

Your reality, as a child of God, is that you have the faith of Jesus already on the inside of you when you invite Him into your life. You can speak how He spoke; believe how He believed and do what He did! You are like Him!

Many times, you focus more on the abilities others possess; their gifts and talents, and many of the things on the outside. If someone sings well, you wish you could sing like them, or if someone has the gift of healing and miraculous signs, you also wish you could have their gifts. The fact is you have the greatest gift of all living inside of you.

While you are busy comparing yourself to others, have you even focused on the Christ who lives inside of you? His endless possibilities that could shine through you? Let's shift our focus. Recognize that the Son of God, the miracle working, Word speaking, healing Jesus lives in you. The abilities He exhibited while on earth, you also have the potential to do as well. As He is limitless, barrierless and boundaryless, so are you, right now, in this world.

Go ahead, take every limit, barrier, and boundary off, and watch how the amazing Son of God will shine through you.

Chapter 21
As He is Filled with Life, So Am I

**But if the Spirit of Him who raised
Jesus from the dead dwells in you, He
who raised Christ from the dead will
also give life to your mortal bodies
through His Spirit who dwells in you.
(Romans 8:11 – NKJV).**

*T*he Holy Spirit continued to speak to me on this theme, showing me that I possess the Giver of Life on the inside of me.

I know many will have a more spiritualized revelation of the above verse, but mine is simple. Christ's resurrection was physical. It was His body that came back to life. The same Spirit who caused the physical body of Jesus Christ to rise, is the same Spirit who lives in my physical body. It therefore means that the Spirit who gives life can revitalize, replenish, and repair my mortal, physical, human body—every cell, every organ, every area of my natural body, can be renewed and pumped with life.

When you are sick, and your body insists on doing the opposite of what the scriptures say, remember to agree with the scriptures. Do not agree with sickness. Proclaim this Word and activate the life-giving ability of the Holy Spirit so He can manifest His healing in your body. You are like Jesus Christ! You have the same Spirit that Jesus had while He was on earth.

Remind yourself of this truth. Speak it!

Chapter 22
Vocabulary Re-Training

Let the word of Christ dwell in you richly in all wisdom... (Colossians 3:16a – KJV).

For the LORD gives wisdom; From His mouth come knowledge and understanding; He stores up sound wisdom for the upright. (Proverbs 2:6-7 – NKJV).

*M*ost babies say their first word sometime between their first 12 to 18 months. However, you will start to hear the early stages of verbal communication shortly after birth. "From birth to three months, babies make sounds. There is smiling and cooing," explained Kaleigh Loeffler, a speech language pathologist in an article for Children's Health. After nine months, babies can understand a few basic words like "No" and "bye-bye." They may also begin to use a wider range of consonant sounds and tones of voice. This is the beginning of our vocabulary, and our vocabulary normally grows as we grow. Your vocabulary is a purely physical tool and is associated with the physical body.

In September 2020, the Holy Spirit impressed the above scriptures in my heart. I know it is important to speak to grow one's vocabulary, but He also showed me that my spiritual vocabulary had to grow. To do this, it had to be re-trained. Not only are we taught words to speak, but those words also shape how we think. Our vocabulary shapes the conversations we have in our minds, and impacts our decisions. I wasn't aware how much my physical surroundings were shaping my life, choices, and thoughts until the Lord showed me that I needed to re-train my vocabulary.

What does that mean? It means learning a new language based on the scriptures; saying what the Word says and not what the world says. The scripture is the language of another Kingdom. As we become part of the Kingdom of God, some of us were never taught that our language and way of speaking must also change in alignment with the language of His Kingdom. This is what the Holy Spirit taught me, **Let the word of Christ dwell in you richly in all wisdom."** **(Colossians 3:16 - NKJV).** Let this Kingdom language dwell in you. When the Word of God dwells in us, our vocabulary will be changed, and we will see the results of what we speak.

God speaks to us, but we must also know how to speak like Him.

Chapter 23
I Should Have Died, But God!

**Then Jesus answered and said to her,
"O woman, great is your faith! Let it be
to you as you desire." And her daughter
was healed from that very hour.
(Matthew 15:28 – NKJV).**

At the age of seven, I was in and out of the hospital, in and out of doctors' offices, and in and out of school. I had missed so many classes at that tender age that it was uncertain whether I could take the examination to move on to high school. My mother's faith was the rock that our family stood on.

Most of my early life was a blur. I was riddled with moments of lucidity and times when I just could not remember what happened. My early memories were in patches because of my fainting spells. In a moment, I was okay and, in a split second, I was out cold. My mother said someone had to always be around me to prevent me from falling and hurting myself if I fainted.

Years of visitation to doctors and countless consultants left them baffled. My sickness mimicked epilepsy in every way, except that I didn't foam at the mouth.

At a Sunday night service, I fainted. My mother took me to the altar at the front of the church cradled in her arms. I was unresponsive. She then whispered a prayer, "Lord, You gave her to me. If it's time for You to take her back, Your will be done." The church was in an uproar, she said. Everyone had known the little girl with the silent epileptic fit. Was she dead?

The prayer intercessors went into action as my mother went back to her seat in tears. They prayed. One person stretched my unresponsive body out on the ground of our little wooden church and called me back to life. There was a nurse among the intercessors, and she checked me for a pulse. There was none. They prayed more. After what seemed like forever, my mother said they heard a gasp. I coughed. They checked the pulse; it was stronger. That Sunday night, what should have been a regular Sunday night church service, became the time the power of the Holy Spirit visited our little wooden church. The people who were present experienced a real-life miracle that night.

I didn't just survive that night, but I was completely healed from any more fainting spells or epileptic sickness. God gave me a second chance that night.

I am here and alive today only because of God's goodness. I should have died, but God!

Chapter 24
Another Miracle Baby

"Before I formed you in the womb, I
knew you; Before you were born, I
sanctified you; I ordained you a prophet
to the nations" (Jeremiah 1:5 – NKJV).

After the birth of our son in 2003, and experiencing the miraculous power of God, we knew we wanted another child. Our plan was always to have our children close in age so they could grow up together.

We were so focused on conceiving our first child, but it was the exact opposite with our second. She was an unplanned surprise! Without much effort, and the same month we had found out about our first child two years earlier, we found out we were pregnant again.

It is fascinating how we women are made up. While each pregnancy is different, there are some common indicators we can use to know we are pregnant long before we get confirmation from a pregnancy test. As we journeyed home from work on January 10, 2005, I remember being so parched. Nothing could quench my thirst. No amount of water I drank all day did anything to refresh me! On the way home, I realized that how parched I was feeling seemed vaguely familiar. I said nothing to my husband. Instead, we stopped at a pharmacy for me to get something to drink. By this time, I had figured out that the way I was feeling was similar to my first pregnancy. While picking up something to drink, I also got a pregnancy test. My husband had no idea what was happening. I couldn't wait to get home.

When we got home, I immediately rushed to the bathroom and got to work with the pregnancy kit. Sure enough, the result was positive, and we were pregnant. I was floored! The Lord favoured us in such a magnificent way that without effort, this time, we were pregnant. After getting over the initial shock, I presented my husband with the result. He was as shocked as I was! After the shock and awe subsided, we began to realize what a blessing God had done for us. Effortlessly, we were pregnant again. Hallelujah!

The pregnancy was a joy. The blessing of having our first child just shy of a year and a half, and expecting another, was pure bliss. I enjoyed the developmental stages, and the first trimester of pregnancy went well.

It was May 2, 2005, a regular day at work, and the workday was stressful, like any other. It wasn't until I popped into the restroom that I realized I had been bleeding or "spotting" as it is called. My mind began to race uncontrollably and hysterically. I kept asking myself, "What is this? What's going on?" Yet, even in the face of my emergency, God was speaking. I heard the instruction, "Go and lie down." I immediately went to a recovery room and laid down.

I called my husband while lying on my back to try and explain what had happened. By this time, I had such a supernatural peace. I called the doctor who said "Marvine, you need to find a quiet place and lie down until you're able to come to my office this afternoon." He had back-to-back appointments and was in-between surgeries. I knew it must have been the Holy Spirit who spoke to me earlier instructing me to lie down. Afterwards, I became so relaxed that I fell asleep.

Yet again, I began to declare over this child as I did over the first child, **"He grants the barren woman a home, Like a joyful mother of children. Praise the LORD!" (Psalm 113:9 – NKJV).** God had done it before for us; He could do it again!

That afternoon, we patiently waited for our appointment to see the doctor. I remembered while lying on the doctor's table how peaceful I felt. As he moved the ultrasound device over my stomach, I noticed a change in his facial features. He had always been a jovial practitioner; that is one of the things we loved about him, but his features changed, and a look of concern was on his face. I could see he was trying to remain calm. He closed the curtain and spoke directly to my husband. "Take her straight to the hospital," he said. "By the time I get there, she must be prepped and ready for surgery. Her cervix is opening and if we don't act quickly, the fetus will abort." This was not the news we were expecting. Our little blessing from God was being aborted; that was not part of the plan!

We followed the doctor's instructions and went straight to the hospital. We didn't go home to get any clothing, or anything else for that matter. By the time we registered and went on to the maternity ward, the nurses had been expecting us. Without delay, I was prepped and ready for surgery. All my work clothes were stripped and had vanished, and I was fully clad in my hospital gown. As I laid there on that hospital bed, we both felt terrified at the speed at which everything was happening. I knew my husband was nervous because this was beyond anything we could have imagined would happen, but he kept his composure. There was nothing else to do at that point, so we prayed and put our trust in God.

The surgery was complete in a few hours. The doctor sutured my cervix for the fetus to remain in place. That was the beginning of a long journey ahead. I remained in the hospital for two weeks after surgery and was only sent home after being given strict instructions to remain in bed for the rest of the pregnancy. "She must only leave the bed for the bathroom," was the direction from the doctor. "Nothing else." That was the beginning of four long months of laying down for the remainder of the pregnancy.

While I spent the time at home, I prayed for and spoke daily to our baby. We later learned that we would be having a girl. Although it was a frightening experience, we knew who the real enemy was, and his purpose was to **"kill, steal and**

destroy." (John 10:10 - NKJV). There was no way we would give up on our pregnancy without putting up a fight! We declared the Word of God daily. We spoke to our baby and told her how God's hand was on her from the womb.

> **"Before I formed you in the womb, I**
> **knew you; Before you were born, I**
> **sanctified you; I ordained you a prophet**
> **to the nations." (Jeremiah 1:5 – NKJV).**

We refused to let go of the Word.

On August 19, 2005, we gave birth to a perfectly beautiful baby girl named Justine. At the time of writing this book, she was seventeen years old.

God can speak to you in your most terrifying moments, but you must listen for His voice!

Please Leave a Review on Amazon

Hey there!

If you have read this far in my book, it means you have heard stories of how God still speaks in the life of believers today.

My personal memoir has been an amazing journey. It is filled with testimonies that magnify Jesus Christ, and I want to share it with the world.

I ask that you be kind enough to leave an honest review of my book on your Amazon portal.

Reviews should only be 1-2 sentences and should take about thirty seconds of your time. It would make a huge difference for me to get this book all over the world.

Thank you for your support.

Marvine

www.ingramcontent.com/pod-product-compliance
Lightning Source LLC
Chambersburg PA
CBHW071100090426
42737CB00013B/2405